Understanding the Purpose of Challenging Behavior:
A Guide to Conducting Functional Assessments

A. James Artesani
University of Maine

Merrill
Prentice Hall

Upper Saddle River, New Jersey
Columbus, Ohio

D1416633

Vice President and Publisher: Jeffery W. Johnston
Acquisitions Editor: Ann Castel Davis
Editorial Assistant: Amy Shough
Production Editor: Kimberly Lundy
Design Coordinator: Robin Chukes
Cover Designer: Diane Lorenzo
Cover Image/photo: © Photodisk, Inc.
Production Manager: Laura Messerly
Director of Marketing: Kevin Flanagan
Marketing Manager: Amy June
Marketing Services Manager: Krista Groshong

10 9 8 7 6 5 4 3 2 1

ISBN: 0-13-032183-4

Preface

I recently had the opportunity to participate in a study that examined the perspectives of principals on problem behavior in schools. The interviews conducted during the study reaffirmed that one of the most pressing issues facing public schools is student behavior. The participants in the study discussed the challenge of problem behavior in terms of the growing number of students exhibiting such behaviors, the increasingly serious nature of the behaviors, and the limited resources many schools have to effectively address such behaviors. This study was conducted in one state; however, the findings were consistent with many larger studies that confirm the significant that challenge student behavior presents to educators. Whether students currently attending America's schools present more of a behavioral challenge than their predecessors remains a hotly debated topic; however, concern for such behavior is clearly evident and warranted. In an effort to respond to these concerns, schools are seeking effective methods to address student behavior. Functional assessment is one of the most effective methods currently available to schools is.

This booklet provides an overview of functional assessment, specifically explaining what functional assessment is and how it can be used as a basis for developing broad support plans as well as specific interventions for students with challenging behavior. While there is a good deal of research supporting the efficiency of functional assessment, this booklet seeks to provide a basic understanding of this process, with practitioners as the primary audience. To this end, the material presented here is written in a style that avoids technical language when possible; however, readers will find that an understanding of basic terms will greatly assist in their understanding of the material. To promote and facilitate further study in this area, a bibliography of research studies, practical articles, and books—as well as Internet resources—is included.

ACKNOWLEDGMENTS

I would like to thank Ann Davis for providing me with the opportunity to write about a topic that I feel is very important to educators and students. I would also like to acknowledge Laura Artesani for her tireless proofreading.

Contents

NOTE: Every effort has been made to provide accurate and current Internet information
in this book. However, the Internet and information posted on it are constantly changing,
so it is inevitable that some of the Internet addresses listed in this textbook will change.

Section I

What Is Functional Assessment?

Functional assessment is a process that leads to a better understanding of why students engage in specific problem behaviors. The information obtained from the assessment is ideally suited to developing behavioral support plans and interventions that result in a variety of positive outcomes for the student. First and foremost, however, functional assessment is a means for understanding the function or purpose of a student's behavior. Functional assessment seeks to answer why a student engages in a particular behavior. Function is often associated with what the student achieves by engaging in the problem behavior: the payoff. The purpose of understanding the function is to identify positive or socially acceptable behaviors the student can use to meet the same function or needs he or she formally met through the problem behaviors. Thus, once the function has been determined, the student can be taught socially appropriate behaviors that serve the same function as the problem behavior.

Understanding why a student engages in problem behavior is critical to the development of a behavioral support plan, but it is only one of the outcomes of functional assessment. In this type of assessment the assessor also examines problem behavior within the natural context that it occurs. Understanding the contextual factors that contribute to challenging behavior provides invaluable information educators can use to effectively address the student's behavior. Functional assessment also examines the personal and family-related issues that may be impacting student behavior.

A number of effective methods and tools have been developed for conducting functional assessments. Depending on which methods and tools are used for the assessment, different amounts and kinds of information can be gathered.

WHAT ASSUMPTIONS ARE MADE ABOUT BEHAVIOR?

Functional assessment is based on the principles of applied behavior analysis. As such, when using functional assessment the assessor must accept certain underlying assumptions (Carr, Levin, McConnachie, Carlson, Kemp, & Smith, 1994; Durand & Crimmins, 1988; O'Neill, Horner, Albin, Sprague, Storey, & Newton, 1997; Reichle & Wacker, 1993).

The primary assumption is that behavior *serves a function* for the individual who exhibits it. That is to say, the behavior is purposeful. It meets a need for the student. A second assumption is that the function is *valid* for the student. The student is using problem behavior to meet a need or serve a function that is meaningful and important to the student. Third, the behavior is *learned* and, as a result, can be unlearned. More specifically, a student can learn to refrain from engaging in a problem behavior, and he or she can also learn new behaviors that serve the same function or purpose as that of the challenging behavior. Fourth, problem behavior is often viewed as a *form of communication*. Students use problem behavior to communicate what they want or do not want. This is most often seen with students who have severe disabilities and lack a formal method of communication that allows them to meet their needs. Fifth, problem behavior results from a lack of basic *social skills*. Many students have reasonably good basic communication skills; however, they may lack the social skills needed to interact effectively with peers and adults. Sixth, problem behavior may be a *source of internal pleasure* for the individual. Behaviors in this category would include such sensory behaviors as finger flicking, rocking, and overeating. Such behaviors provide sensory gratification to the person engaging in them. Sensory behaviors can also serve the purpose of heightening or lowering one's state of arousal. Finally, problem behavior can be something a student does when he or she does not know what else to do. Students sometimes engage in what appears to be a pointless activity because they lack an alternative. In such cases these behaviors occur as an alternative to doing

8

nothing. Once they are engaged, however, such behaviors sometimes evolve into other forms of reinforcement.

Problem behavior often serves *multiple purposes or functions* and may require a variety of interventions. For example, John is a student who has difficulty with math. During math he engages in mildly disruptive behavior. His teacher responds by giving the student a verbal reprimand and a three-minute period of time out. This response provides the student with removal from his math, an activity he does not like. In English class John sits next to Sarah, a young woman he would like to date. John notices that Sarah smiles and laughs when he makes jokes in class. Although his teacher tries to discourage this behavior, John continues to make jokes because he finds Sarah's attention highly reinforcing. In the math example the function of John's behavior is escape, but in English the function is attention.

Another way to think about problem behavior from the functional perspective is that although it may be *maladaptive* in appearance it can also be considered *adaptive* because it provides the student with a means for meeting a particular need or purpose. The problem behaviors are labeled maladaptive because they may involve actions that are not sanctioned by society or are considered in some way deviant. From the functional perspective, however, labeling behaviors as deviant or socially unacceptable does not lead to a solution. We know that maladaptive behaviors typically need to be corrected, but knowing the function tells us how we might go about changing them.

WHAT ARE THE GOALS OF FUNCTIONAL ASSESSMENT?

There are a variety of methods and tools for conducting functional assessment. Regardless of how the assessment is completed, a thorough functional assessment should address the following goals:

1. Identification of personal or family issues that affect behavior.
2. Identification of health or medical concerns that affect behavior.
3. Identification of the specific environmental variables that predict the occurrence and nonoccurrence of problem behavior.
4. Identification of the consequences that serve to reinforce or maintain the occurrence of problem behavior.
5. Identification of the function or purpose(s) of the problem behavior.

This case study will illustrate the goals addressed in a functional assessment.

Case Study: Michael

Michael is a student who is typically irritable, short-tempered and often complains about not feeling well. His teacher believes he has allergies that have not been addressed by a doctor. During a call home, Michael's mother divulged that she is a single parent who recently lost her job. She also lost her health benefits and is concerned about the cost of medications and visits to the doctor. In school, Michael often refuses to complete his work. His teacher responds to this refusal by insisting that the work be completed or Michael will lose recess time. Michael typically responds to this directive by destroying his work materials. Michael is then sent to the office for his offense.

Functional assessment can assist Michael's teacher in a number of ways in understanding why he refuses to do his math. Often, the first area addressed under functional assessment is the events that set the stage for problem behavior to occur. In Michael's case, his teacher may ask the school nurse to address the allergy problem with Michael's mother. The teacher may also ask the guidance counselor to look into the personal stresses Michael and his mother are experiencing at home. Addressing these family issues will make additional behavioral programs more effective. In the school arena, potential environmental variables, such as the level of work Michael is being asked to complete, the kind of directions his teacher gives him, or the type of assistance Michael may need, would likely be examined as well. Environmental factors are often referred to as *predictors* of problem behaviors. We will discuss predictors in more detail later in this booklet.

A second area examined in a functional assessment is the consequences that serve to reinforce or maintain the problem behaviors. In Michael's case his behavior results in the consequence of being sent to the office. While this may sound like a punishment to most people, it may be a form of reinforcement for Michael. In fact, given the recurrence of Michael's behavior, one might make the assumption that he would rather leave the room than do his assignments. Michael's teacher will definitely want to rethink that strategy. This leads to the fifth goal of functional assessment: obtaining an understanding of the function of the problem behavior. In Michael's case the purpose appears to be escape from difficult schoolwork.

There are a number of goals one might seek when beginning a functional assessment; however, at the heart of the process is a desire to understand the function or purpose of the challenging behavior. It is this goal that sets functional assessment apart from other ecological or behavioral assessment approaches.

Section II

Why Conduct Functional Assessments?

There are many reasons to use functional assessment in school settings. A few of the most important reasons are presented in this section.

FUNCTIONAL ASSESSMENT IS VERSATILE

Functional assessment can be used with a variety of behaviors and is particularly useful for serious behaviors that exist for a variety of complex reasons. It can be used to address chronic low intensity behaviors such as speaking to classmates during silent reading periods and minor arguments between peers. It is also useful and even more of a necessity to conduct functional assessments with serious behaviors that are often complex and difficult to understand. Relatively minor problem behaviors can often be assessed through functional assessment methods that require a minimal amount of time and effort on the part of the teacher or evaluator. A thorough functional assessment, however, is a prerequisite for developing effective interventions for serious problem behaviors such as physical aggression, self-injurious behavior, sexual harassment, substance abuse and destruction of property.

Functional assessment uncovers variables that contribute to the problem behavior. Through functional assessment educators can identify family, personal (e.g., biological or physiological), and school-related environmental variables that predict the occurrence of problem behavior.

This information can be used to create home and school environments that result in a reduction of problem behaviors and an increase of positive behaviors. In fact, teachers are responsible for, and many are adept at setting up, environments that promote positive social/emotional growth as well as academic development. A clear understanding of individual student needs is paramount to developing an environment that supports learning. This is the first step in using functional assessment data to develop supportive environments for students with problem behaviors.

Functional assessment allows teachers to teach replacement behaviors. Once the function of the behavior has been identified, educators can use their knowledge to teach new, more socially appropriate behaviors that meet the same function or need as the problem behavior. This process significantly reduces the student's need to engage in challenging behavior to meet his or her needs.

Functional assessment fosters the use of positive supports and interventions. The application of functional assessment to school and home settings has in large part occurred simultaneously with the growing trend in the use of positive approaches to problem behavior. In fact, the 1999 amendments to the Individuals with Disabilities Education Act require that functional assessment data be used to create positive intervention and support plans. Data from functional assessments lends itself to the development of positive behavioral supports and interventions that go beyond simply reducing problem behavior. Data from a functional assessment can be used to create a supportive environment in which the student can develop new behaviors and be successful in a variety of areas.

Functional assessment promotes positive relationships between students and educators. Functional assessment provides a gateway to education-based approaches to problem behavior. It is important to remember that the evaluator is not seeking to discount the needs or functions the student is meeting through his or her problem behaviors. Instead, the purpose of identifying the function is so that an alternative behavior can be identified and taught that meets the same need as the problem behavior. These educationally valid approaches rely on positive, instructional interactions between school personnel and the student. Teaching students new ways to meet their needs empowers the student and fosters a more positive relationship between educator and student.

Functional assessment is required by the Individuals with Disabilities Education Act (IDEA). The 1997 Amendments to the Individuals with Disabilities Education Act (IDEA) mandate that when disciplinary action is taken against a student receiving special education, educators responsible for developing individualized education programs (IEPs) must conduct a functional behavioral assessment. Functional assessment is specifically warranted when the disciplinary action involves a change of placement, such as suspension from school for more than 10 days. As part of this process, the team is required to make a *manifest determination*. The purpose of this determination is to ascertain whether the behavior leading to the disciplinary action was under the control of the student or whether it was a manifestation of the student's disability. Two decisions need to be made. First, was the behavior related to educational or non-educational concerns? If the behavior impedes the education of the student with a disability or other students, it is likely to be educational in nature. Second, the team must determine if the student's disability impaired his or her ability to understand the impact and consequences of the behavior. In other words, did the student's disability impair his or her ability to control the behavior? If the answer to these questions is yes, policies and rules related to special education and compliance with IDEA apply. Interpreting Federal legislation is a complicated task. Further information on the requirements for functional assessment under the 1997 Amendments to IDEA can be found at the Internet sites listed below.

http://www.air-dc.org/cecp/resources/problembehavior/introduction.htm

http://coehp.idbsu.edu/mbarrer/TET497/discipline%20procedures%20under%20idea%2097/ppframe.htm

Section III

When Should Functional Assessment Be Conducted?

Functional assessment is often implemented when a student's behavior is ongoing and impedes his or her educational and/or social development or that of other students. It may also be implemented when a student breaks school or other accepted norms for behavior.

Functional assessment is also used when a student's behavior does not respond to classroom management strategies proven to be effective in addressing routine forms of problem behavior. In some cases it is used for behaviors that have proven resistant to change despite the initial use of individualized behavior programs.

Research has demonstrated the critical role functional assessment can play in effectively addressing serious problem behaviors including such behaviors as physical aggression, verbal harassment, self-injurious behavior, and property destruction. Many of these studies have addressed behaviors that are of high frequency and high intensity. In many cases, serious problem behaviors result from a complex mix of personal and environmental factors. An example of this would be a child who has a mental health disorder, is unsuccessful in school, both academically and socially, and has a difficult home life. A thorough functional assessment, while not leading to simple or easy solutions, can provide information that will lead to a better understanding of how these issues are affecting the child's behavior as well as strategies to address them in a comprehensive way.

Although functional assessment can be a time-intensive process, a wide array of tools and methods is available to educators wishing to use this approach. The various tools and methods make it possible to conduct such an assessment in a relatively short period of time or without consuming significant school resources. Suggestions to guide the selection of tools and methods are presented in the next section.

Section IV

Understanding the Basics: Terms and Concepts

Functional assessment can be a very technical process. It is based on principles of behavioral psychology, and there is a good deal of scientific research that supports its effectiveness. Not surprisingly, the professional literature often includes some technical language. As mentioned earlier, this book is designed for practitioners who may or may not be familiar with language surrounding functional assessment. Understanding the terms and concepts presented in this section that are closely associated with functional assessment will lead to a better understanding of how and why this assessment process works. This is important for two reasons. First, educators who understand the principles, concepts, and terminology of functional assessment will be better prepared to utilize functional assessment strategies. Second, such knowledge will allow the assessor to conduct a more in-depth and sophisticated analysis of the assessment findings. In addition, most readers will recall many of these terms from introductory psychology courses. The terms and concepts will be presented in the context of the goals of the functional assessment process presented earlier. Examples from school settings will be used to illustrate each term or concept.

SETTING EVENTS

As discussed in the case study on Michael, one goal of a functional assessment is to identify events in the environment that lead to the problem behavior. Environmental factors that contribute to the problem behavior but occur somewhat distant from the actual occurrence of the behavior are referred to as setting events (Foster-Johnson & Dunlap, 1993; O'Neill et. al., 1997). Setting events can be people, places, environmental conditions, activities, or health issues that lead to the occurrence of the problem behavior. They may occur at home before the student reaches school, on the bus or walk to school or while the student is in school. Such events are often present when the behavior takes place. For example, heat, fatigue, and noise may be setting events that contribute to a student's disruptive behavior. For the purpose of clarity, setting events will be divided into personal and family factors, and school factors.

Personal and Family Factors

There are many personal and family-related factors that can contribute to problem behavior. Family factors can include chronic conditions such as

- abuse,
- neglect,
- poverty, and
- poor nutrition

or more current events, such as

- divorce,
- loss of work for parents,
- marital strife, or
- a death in the family.

It is important to note that personal/family concerns do not have to be as overt as those mentioned. They can also be subtle and produce gradual effects on the student's behavior. Personal factors can include

- chronic or temporary health concerns,
- medications,
- neurological disorders,
- lack of sleep, or

- mental health issues.

Educators often feel that family and personal factors are beyond their control. This may be true in many instances, but the future success of school-based interventions will be impacted by the degree to which family and personal factors can be resolved.

School-related Environmental Factors

Many factors can lead to problem behaviors in the school setting as well. These factors include people, events, times of day, and activities that, like family and personal issues, increase the likelihood that the problem behavior will occur. Examples of environmental factors that can contribute to challenging behavior include the following:

Classroom Factors
- size of room
- density of people
- temperature
- lighting
- high levels of carbon dioxide and other air quality issues
- high noise levels
- visual and auditory distractions

Curriculum and Instruction Factors
- unclear directions
- lack of organization
- lack of predictability in schedule
- activities the student dislikes
- unclear expectations for quality or quantity of work
- curriculum that is perceived as irrelevant
- inadequate assistance when needed
- frequent or disorganized transitions

These are just a few of the many potential environmental contributors to appropriate and problem behaviors in school settings. Like personal and family factors, school related variables may not lead directly to the occurrence of the problem behaviors, but they do set the stage for them to occur.

Antecedents

Antecedents, like setting events, are environmental factors that occur directly before the occurrence of the problem behavior. They are often referred to as environmental "triggers". Like setting events, antecedents are environmental factors that lead to the behavior; the difference is that the behavior is actually triggered by the antecedent. Examples of antecedents include the following:

- argumentative tone of voice
- being told "no" in response to a question
- having a desired item or activity taken away
- being teased or verbally harassed
- being physically attacked
- being given a directive by a teacher that is not liked

There are many potential antecedents or triggers for appropriate and problem behaviors. How a student responds to a given antecedent can vary depending on the presence of certain setting events. The evaluator should search for patterns in the effects of specific antecedents on student behavior.

Predictors

Personal and family factors, environmental factors, and antecedents are often referred to as predictors of problem behaviors. An example will help clarify the connection between personal or family factors and environmental factors and antecedents.

Scenario: Mr. Smith

Mr. Smith likes his days to unfold in an orderly fashion. He does not like surprises or deviations from his routine. This morning Mr. Smith awoke with a sore back that made routine tasks such as getting dressed a painful chore. He then went into the kitchen for his coffee and oatmeal. He was quite upset to find the power had gone out in his house. Not only did his coffee maker and stove not work, thus depriving him of his breakfast, but also his clocks had stopped and he was sixty minutes late for work. On the way to work Mr. Smith encountered heavy traffic that put him further behind schedule. By the time he got to his office Mr. Smith was angry and frustrated, but so far he had managed to maintain his composure. Shortly after Mr. smith sat down behind his desk, a student came by his office. She told him that she had not had time to finish her assignments and that he should have given them more time to complete the work in the first place. Mr. Smith bristled and then exploded. He told his student in a loud, angry voice that she had better finish the assignment on time and be more responsible in the future.

Let's connect the events of Mr. Smith's behavioral episode to factors we have been discussing.

Personal Factors	Environmental Factors	Antecedent	Behavior
Sore back	Power out	Student late	Yelled at
	No coffee	with work	student
	No oatmeal	Accusation of	
	Heavy traffic	poorly scheduled	
	Late for work	due date	

Of course, in Mr. Smith's case his behavior is the result of an atypical array of difficult events. This is a very different scenario from the chronic problem behaviors educators must address. In school settings, problem behavior is often characterized by a variety of environmental factors combined with students who often do not have effective coping strategies. This is a recipe for chronic problem behavior.

Identifying environmental factors that contribute to problem behavior is vital, but identifying environmental factors and antecedents that do not contribute to the problem behavior is important as well. Knowing what factors contribute to positive or socially appropriate behaviors for a student is very useful in designing environments that support expected behaviors.

CONSEQUENCES

Understanding what predicts the occurrence of problem behaviors is an important outcome of the assessment, but identifying the events that occur following or as a result of the behavior is just as important. These events or responses to the behavior are called consequences, and they can serve to reinforce or punish the behavior. Consequences that reinforce the behavior are also called maintaining reinforcers because they increase or maintain the likelihood that the behavior will occur again. Consequences in the form of reinforcement for expected behavior and punishment for problem behavior have been used for many years in education. Teachers and parents use various forms of consequences every day. Traditionally, however, consequences have been used as part of the intervention plan. In functional assessment they are a critical piece of the assessment process because they tell us why the student is engaging in the behavior.

FUNCTION

Consequences are important in the functional assessment process because they tell us what is motivating the problem behavior. Through an analysis of the consequences that follow problem behavior we can determine the function of the behavior. In a functional assessment process, the function of behavior is divided into two broad categories: to obtain internal or external reinforcement or to escape from internal or external punishment. Obtaining reinforcement in the form of sensory stimulation, attention, or a tangible item is referred to as positive reinforcement. It is positive because the student has obtained something he or she wanted. Escape from something the student does not want is referred to as negative reinforcement. In other words, the student is reinforced because her behavior allows her to avoid or escape something she finds aversive. The terms *positive* and *negative* do not imply something being good or bad: Positive simply means a desired reinforcement was obtained, and negative refers to reinforcement being derived from the removal or avoidance of an undesired stimulus or situation. A few brief examples of positive and negative reinforcers are listed below to clarify these terms.

Positive Reinforcement (Obtaining)
- Work hard to obtain money
- Steal to obtain food
- Study to obtain praise
- Make noise to obtain attention
- Finish homework to obtain TV time

Negative Reinforcement (Escaping or Avoiding)
- Cover ears to avoid loud noise
- Refuse to eat to avoid bad tasting food

- Work hard to avoid reprimands
- Walk home using a different route to avoid teasing
- Complain to avoid difficult tasks

Notice that in the examples for both positive and negative reinforcement the behavior is reinforced because the purpose is achieved, that the function of the behavior is met. Thus, reinforcement—either by obtaining what one wants (positive) or escaping what one does not want (negative)—increases the likelihood that the behavior will occur again.

The following examples show how problem behavior is affected by maintaining reinforcers in each of the function areas.

Obtaining Internal Stimulation

Example 1

Behavior: John, a student with autism, often rocks back and forth in his chair

Maintaining reinforcer: John receives positive reinforcement in the form of sensory stimulation. His teacher has observed that this calms him down.

Function: To obtain internal stimulation

Example 2

Behavior: Tom drinks six cups of coffee per day.

Maintaining reinforcer: Tom receives internal stimulation from the caffeine in the coffee.

Function: To obtain internal stimulation from drinking coffee

Obtaining External Stimulation—Attention

Example 1

Behavior: During independent work periods Kathy often talks with her classmates.

Maintaining reinforcer: Kathy receives positive reinforcement in the form of attention from her teacher who addresses this behavior by coming over and telling Kathy to work quietly and not bother her classmates.

Function: To obtain attention from peers.

Example 2

Behavior: Jack wrote a bomb threat on a bathroom mirror at school.

Maintaining reinforcer: Jack received positive reinforcement in the form of attention from peers who told him it would be "cool" if he wrote the threat.

Function: To obtain attention from peers.

Obtaining External Stimulation—Tangible

Example 1

Behavior: Between classes Charley broke into Sam's locker and stole his new backpack.

Maintaining reinforcer: Charley received positive reinforcement by getting the tangible item (backpack) he coveted.

Function: To obtain a tangible item

Example 2

Behavior: Kate cried because she wanted a snack that she could not have.

Maintaining reinforcer: The teacher let Kate eat a cookie from her lunchbox. Kate received the item she wanted. She received positive reinforcement by obtaining the cookie.

Function: To obtain a tangible item.

Escaping Internal Stimulation

Example 1

Behavior: Joan scratches her arms and legs, sometimes making them bleed.

Maintaining reinforcer: Scratching relieves the itching caused by a skin condition. Joan receives a form of negative reinforcement because she escapes the itching.

Function: To escape internal stimulation.

Example 2

Behavior: James screams and slaps the side of his head when he is hungry.

Maintaining reinforcer: Slapping his head results in someone providing James with food that removes the hunger. James receives a form of negative reinforcement because he escapes being hungry.

Function: To escape internal stimulation.

Escaping External Stimulation

Example 1

Behavior: Tara often skips social studies class.

Maintaining reinforcer: Tara receives negative reinforcement from the external stimulation provided in the social studies class. She is able to escape by skipping social studies class.

Function: To escape external stimulation.

Example 2

Behavior: Carl punched a student who was teasing him.

Maintaining reinforcer: Carl was reinforced because the student stopped teasing him after the punch. He received negative reinforcement because he escaped the teasing.

Function: To escape external stimulation

Reducing the motivation of problem behavior to two sources, to obtain and to escape may seem to be an inadequate explanation for complex behavior. It is important to remember that functional assessment also seeks to identify personal and family related factors that contribute to students' problem behaviors.

Even in complex cases, maintaining reinforcers play a critical role in the continued presence of problem behaviors. They illustrate what the student is deriving from the behavior. Thus they are key to understanding the function of a problem behavior.

REPLACEMENT BEHAVIORS

Understanding the relationship between maintaining reinforcers and the function of a student's behavior is important because, as mentioned at the beginning of the booklet, understanding the function of behavior is the primary purpose of functional assessment. Educators can use their knowledge of the function of a student's behavior to identify alternative, or replacement, behaviors that can be taught to the student. These new behaviors, if carefully chosen, should meet the same function as the problem behavior. Thus, replacement behaviors provide the student with a socially appropriate means to meet their needs without having to resort to problem behaviors. The following is an example of a replacement behavior.

Behavior: Glory often gets angry when she has trouble with schoolwork she finds difficult.

Maintaining reinforcer: Seeing Glory's anger, her teacher comes over and provides assistance.

Function: To obtain assistance from the teacher.
Replacement behavior: Glory's teacher is encouraging Glory to ask for help before she gets to the point where she is angry.

This section has focused on the terminology and concepts necessary to understand how the functional assessment process works. The example below uses one case scenario to link together the major concepts covered in the preceding discussion.

Scenario: Angela

Angela came to school very angry. Her parents had been having a heated argument, and they both turned their anger on Angela shortly before she left the house. Angela's first class was history—a subject she felt was a waste of her time and that was taught by a teacher with whom she did not get along. Angela and the history teacher had a history of disagreements about her lack of interest and effort in this class. Shortly after arriving in class, Angela's history teacher told her that her shirt, which contained a sexually explicit slogan on the back, was in very poor taste and that she must go and change it immediately. Angela responded by yelling at the teacher and refusing to change the shirt. Her friends laughed and cheered Angela's defiance. The history teacher told Angela to go to the office.

Family/personal factors: Arguing at home between parents and between Angela and her parents.

Environmental factors: Nonpreferred history class, teacher with whom Angela had past disagreements.

Antecedent: Verbal reprimand by the history teacher concerning the shirt.

Behavior: Angela yelled at the teacher and refused to change her shirt.

Consequence: Angela was sent to the office. Angela was also cheered by her friends.

Maintaining reinforcers:
Negative reinforcement—escape from class
Positive reinforcement—attention and praise from peers

Function: Negative reinforcement by avoiding her history class; positive reinforcement in the form of laughs and cheers (attention) from her peers.

Replacement behavior: Improved social skills. Angela needs to learn that she can solve her differences of opinion and perhaps even get into a different history class without yelling.

It is important to note that much of the above scenario is based on a certain amount of speculation. Based on one scenario or behavioral incident, an evaluator cannot be sure how much the arguing at home influences Angela's behavior at school. One also cannot know with certainty the function of Angela's behavior. It appears likely that negative and positive reinforcement was at work, but it would be premature to assume that conclusion based on one behavioral episode. As will be discussed in the next section, functional assessment involves searching the assessment data for patterns in predictors, behaviors, and consequences before drawing conclusions or making explanations about a student's behavior.

The terminology associated with functional assessment may not be part of the daily language used by most educators; however, the benefits of understanding these terms should be clear. Terms and concepts such as antecedent, predictor, maintaining reinforcer, and function help one understand the assumptions and theoretical basis upon which functional assessment works. Once understood, the language of functional assessment facilitates one's understanding of the variables influencing problem behavior, why such behavior occurs, and how educators can address it. A series of more complete case studies illustrating functional assessment outcomes can be found in the Appendix.

Section V

How is a Functional Assessment Completed?

WHO MAY CONDUCT A FUNCTIONAL ASSESSMENT?

Functional assessments can be conducted by a variety of individuals. No special licensing is required; however, a thorough understanding of the behavioral principles that functional assessment is built upon is critical to a meaningful assessment. The assessment procedures can range from fairly simple to quite sophisticated. Obviously the more training, experience, and background one has with functional assessment and behavioral theory, the more sophisticated one can be in the design and methods used to conduct the assessment.

A five-phase process (Figure 5.1) to guide a functional assessment is presented in this section (an optional sixth phase is also described). Some phases have number of steps, but the specific assessment tools and methods used to complete each phase are flexible. Thus, either an experienced behavioral evaluator or someone just getting started can follow this process

---
Phases and Steps in Conducting Functional Assessments

Phase 1:   Articulate the Problem Behavior

        Step 1. Describe the behavior.
        Step 2. Determine if and why the behavior is a
            problem behavior.
        Step 3. Identify how often and for how long the
            behavior occurs.

Phase 2:   Conduct Functional Assessment Interviews

Phase 3:   Conduct Functional Assessment Observations

Phase 4:   Get the Most Out of the Data

Phase 5:   Develop Plausible Hypotheses or Explanations for the

                Occurrence of the Problem Behavior

Phase 6:   Conduct a Functional Analysis (Optional)

Figure 5.1   Process of Functional Assessment

CONDUCTING A FUNCTIONAL ASSESSMENT
Phase 1. Articulate the Problem Behavior
Step 1. Describe the behavior

Kaplan (1995) refers to this step as pinpointing the behavior of concern. One might ask the questions, "What is the behavior?" and "What does it look like when it happens?" O'Neill, et al. (1997) suggest that assessors describe the behavior by using terms that are precise and highly descriptive; this is commonly referred to as the topography of the behavior. Sometimes a student may exhibit a variety of behaviors that can be categorized under a broader heading. For example, a student may invade another student's personal space, lean over them, clench their fists, frown, and speaking loudly, tell the other student they are going to beat them up. Educators may categorize such behaviors as bullying. In this scenario there are a number of behaviors that occur together. Similarly, the term "temper tantrum" is often used to describe certain types of student behavior. Such behavior typically includes a number of discrete behaviors including verbal and physical actions. Sometimes these behaviors occur in a chain that begins with fairly minor, less obtrusive behaviors that quickly escalate to highly disruptive and potentially dangerous behaviors. It is important that the discrete behaviors that make up the behavioral episode be identified so that the specific characteristics of the behavior are known and can be observed and addressed consistently by everyone carrying out the program.

Another similar example involves a male student who makes a variety of inappropriate sexual comments to female students. Such behaviors may be categorized as verbal or sexual harassment. Again, if such general categories are used it is important that a clear delineation of the discrete behaviors that constitute such harassment is made so that everyone involved with the student's program will know what behaviors are being addressed. This type of specificity will also prove helpful in developing a highly individualized and specific intervention plan. General and specific examples of behavioral descriptions are presented in Figure 5.2.

Step 2. Determine if and why the behavior is a problem behavior

This step addresses the question "What is the rationale for changing this behavior?" Before engaging in time-consuming assessments and behavioral programming, it is helpful to examine the significance of the problem behavior. Questions to consider include:

Is the behavior physically harmful to the student or to other students or adults?

Does the behavior disrupt or impede the education of the student in question or his or her peers?

Does the behavior cause undue stress, or is it threatening to other students or staff?

Does the behavior result in a loss or destruction of property?

A second question that should be addressed is: "What socially valid reasons support changing this behavior?"It is useful from a practical standpoint, and ethically appropriate to examine the social validity of changing a student's behavior. Behaviors that should be changed typically violate local community and/or school standards for

Categories of Problem Behaviors	Examples of Specific Behaviors
Physical aggression against person or property	• Hits other students with closed fist • Punches peers and adults • Pulls hair of other students • Tears pages out of textbooks • Pulls glasses and jewelery from adults • Writes on desktops and walls
Self-injurious behavior	• Slaps side of own head with open palm, sometimes leaving bruises • Hits forehead on desk and tabletops
Verbal harassment	• Tells other students he is going to beat them up • Swears at other students
Non-compliant behaviors	• Says "no" in a loud voice • Puts head on desk and ignores teachers' directions

Figure 5.2   Descriptions of Problem Behaviors

what is considered appropriate behavior. While people may have differing points of view concerning what constitutes appropriate and inappropriate behavior, schools are encouraged to develop expectations for behavior that reflect community standards and are readily understood by staff and students. The school is then responsible for modeling, teaching, and sometimes enforcing those expectations. Each student and staff member is responsible for meeting those behavioral expectations. Prior to deciding whether a behavior should be changed, school personnel should consider whether the behavior in question is violating school norms and expectations. The point here is to make sure that educators are viewing student behavior through a broader perspective than their own personal opinions, values, and expectations.

Sociocultural issues unique to a student's background should also be considered prior to labeling a behavior maladaptive, problematic, or inappropriate. Educators should ask themselves if the student's behavior is a violation of behavioral standards, or if it is more a reflection of the individual student's cultural background.

Step 3. Identify how often and for how long the behavior occurs

In an effort to more clearly define the behavior, it is necessary to obtain a baseline consisting of the *frequency* of the behavior (how often occurs)

Date: 5/13/2000
Student: Carolyn
Behavior: Leaves the classroom

Time	Frequency	Total
8:00-9:00	////	4
9:00-10:00	//	2
10:00-11:00	/	1
12:00-1:00	///	3

Figure 5.3   Sample Frequency Recording

and the *duration* of the behavior (how long is lasts). An important function of baseline data is that it provides a measure by which future changes in behavior can be compared after the behavioral supports and intervention have been implemented.

Frequency can be tallied using a simple table such as the one shown in Figure 5.3. Each occurrence of the behavior is recorded by marking a slash or checkmark in the corresponding time slot. Some teachers use a golf or umpire's "clicker" to record each behavioral event.

Date: 3/17/2000
Student: Laura
Behavior: Calls out answer without raising hand

Time	Frequency	Minutes	Rate
8:00-8:15	/////	15	0.33
9:00-9:15	//	15	0.13
10:00-10:30	////	30	0.13
11:00-11:15	////	15	0.26
12:00-12:30	///////	30	0.23

Figure 5.4   Sample Rate Recording

It is important to remember that using consistent time intervals allows the evaluator to establish the *rate* at which the behavior occurs. For example, Samantha engages in pinching other students eight times on Monday, five times on Tuesday, seven times on Wednesday and once on Thursday and Friday. It is then discovered that Samantha was observed for only 30 minutes on Thursday and Friday. Needless to say, trying to identify the rate at which Samantha's behavior occurs without considering the length of time for which it was observed would be misleading. An example of rate recording is found in Figure 5.4.

A stopwatch can be used to measure the duration of a given behavior. Some teachers find it easier to use a running stopwatch that is clicked on when the behavior occurs and off when it ends. The watch is not reset after each incidence. The total time present on the watch at the end of the day or specific interval of time such as a class period is recorded.

Recording the duration of each separate behavioral event, however, is advantageous in that it also provides the frequency of the behavior. For example, Ralph's teacher records the duration of each episode of Ralph arguing with his peers. Adding up the duration of each episode and dividing by the number of episodes provides the average duration of each instance of arguing. Counting each incidence also provides a frequency count. Figure 5.5 displays the duration of each episode as well as the frequency.

Date: 3/13/2000
Student: Emily
Behavior: Arguing

Time	Duration Per Incident (minutes)	Total Duration (minutes)	Frequency
8:00-9:00	2.15, 1.00, 3.10	15	0.33
9:00-10:00	1.50, 3.00	15	0.13
10:00-11:00	3.00, 2.20, 1.20, 3.25	30	0.13
11:00-12:00	3.15, 2.20, 1.00, 4.00, 3.30	15	0.26

Figure 5.5   Sample Frequency and Duration Recording

Phase 2: Conducting Functional Assessment Interviews

Functional assessments are typically completed through interviews or questionnaires and direct observation. A number of excellent assessment tools and procedures have been developed to assist educators in this process (see Additional Resources). Not surprisingly, some of these methods are quite sophisticated and can be time-consuming; other formats are much simpler to use and require much less of a time commitment. Educators should realize, however, that as one moves toward simpler, less time-consuming methods, he or she runs the risk of obtaining less complete information about the student's behavior. In some cases this is not problematic because the behavior is not very complicated or serious and the teacher may be looking for data to confirm what he or she already believes to be the case based on his or her day-to-day work with the student.

There is no hard and fast rule for choosing the right functional assessment method, but generally, the more serious and complex the behavior, the more sophisticated and precise the assessment process needs to be. Educators should keep in mind that serious and complex behaviors typically require more of their time and effort anyway, so conducting a thorough functional assessment may save time and energy and produce more effective results for everyone involved (including the student) in the long run. Guidelines for choosing methods and materials are presented in Figure 5.6.

Interviews are a common method for gathering information concerning student behavior. It should be noted that tools for conducting interviews could also be used as questionnaires. Generally interviews and questionnaires used in functional assessment are one and the same. In some instances an outside consultant might use a particular assessment tool to interview various staff and family members about a student's behavior. In these types of situations the questions are presented in an interview style. The same tool can usually be used as a questionnaire when filled out by a group of teachers who are conducting the assessment themselves. The functional assessment handbook developed by O'Neill et al. (1997) and the Motivation Assessment Scale (MAS) developed by Durand and Crimmins (1988) are prime examples of such tools. Whether used as a questionnaire or an interview, the purpose is the same: to gather information about the student's behavior within the contexts in which it does and does not occur. Questionnaires may consist of relatively brief Likert-type questions or more lengthy open-ended questions. The MAS (Durand & Crimmins, 1988) is a good example of a Likert-type format that provides insight into the motivation or function of a given behavior. The MAS provides numerical scores that coincide with the functional areas of Tangible, Attention, Sensory, and Escape.

Choosing Methods and Materials for a Functional Assessment

1. Choose a method that you understand and will be able to implement. Some questionnaires include questions that concern concepts which may not be familiar to the evaluator. Some observation sheets require a good deal of practice before the evaluator becomes adept at using them. Many functional assessment tools and procedures are most effectively used when the evaluator has at least a basic understanding of the concepts around which the tool is designed and the methods required to use it effectively. For example, it is helpful to understand the basic principles of behavioral theory to later understand how consequences may serve to reinforce or punish behavior.

2. Use methods that make sense considering the evaluator's other work responsibilities and time commitments. Some observation instruments require vigilant observation of a student's behavior. This is often not possible for most teachers unless they have access to additional personnel to assist with either teaching or data collection responsibilities. If resources for collecting data are limited, a less intensive method should be chosen. For example, the demands of an elementary classroom might make it difficult for a teacher to collect data on high frequency behaviors. The teacher would need temporary assistance from a co-teacher, educational assistant, parent, or student teacher. If such assistance is not available, a less demanding process may be required.

3. If the problem behavior is fairly mild in nature (i.e., talking out in class, minor disturbances of classroom routine) and/or is triggered and maintained by a small number of school and home factors, a simpler assessment process may be more time efficient and informative.

4. If the behavior is serious in nature (i.e., physical aggression, substance abuse) and/or complex (i.e., is triggered and maintained by a variety of school and home factors) a more intensive process should be chosen to allow an effective assessment.

Figure 5.6 Conducting a functional assessment interview.

In contrast, O'Neill et al. (1997) created a significantly more involved interview format, as published in Functional Assessment and Program Development for Problem Behavior: A Practical Handbook. His process goes into much greater depth concerning environmental factors, medical/physiological considerations, and functional communication skills. In complex cases the evaluator may choose to use the O'Neill format as the primary questionnaire or interview and then utilize the MAS to validate his or her assumptions, particularly concerning the function of the student's behavior. Carr et al. (1994) also developed a highly regarded process that is systematic and thorough, yet very applicable to educational settings and accessible to educators with little experience in the functional assessment process.

Phase 3: Conducting Functional Assessment Observations

Direct observation of student behavior can serve two purposes. First, it can be used as the primary means of conducting a functional assessment. Second, it can be used along with an interview process to provide two methods for collecting data on a student's behavior. Generally, it is considered good practice to conduct both interviews and observations. One benefit of using both is that you may gather useful data via the observation that did not surface during the interview, or vice versa. For example, during the observation the evaluator may note that the tone of the teacher's voice or how close she is in proximity to the student influences a student's willingness to follow the teacher's directions. Such information may not have surfaced during the interview process. The likelihood of this type of scenario increases when one considers that the interview often consists of a questionnaire filled out by informants such as the student's teacher or parents. While the teacher and the parents may have a great deal of information to provide in the assessment process, they may be too close to the situation to observe important details of their own behavior and how it is affecting the student's behavior. Second, having two methods of collecting data allows the assessor to check the validity of the assumptions and explanations made about the function of the behavior and the impact of specific environmental events. This concern is illustrated in the following scenario.

Scenario: Katie

During interviews, Katie's teacher informed the evaluator that she ignores Katie's behavior when she engages in disruptive behavior to gain attention. During observations, however, the

40

evaluator noted that when Katie engaged in disruptive behavior her teacher often made direct eye contact in the form of a stern frown. Such a response could be quite reinforcing to Katie.

Observation of such a response would be inconsistent with the teacher's claim of ignoring the behavior. It might also be noted during the observation that other students sometimes verbally reprimand Katie when she disrupts them. This would suggest that her teacher and her classmates are actually reinforcing Katie when she disrupts the class.

There are many different ways of conducting direct observations of student behavior. Three methods are presented below in the order that this author would recommend their use.

Scatterplot

The scatterplot, developed by Touchette, MacDonald, & Langer (1985), is a valuable tool that illustrates when behavior occurs and when it does not occur. Squares that correspond to the time of day and the day of the week on the scatterplot are filled in if the behavior occurs during a given time interval. The behavior could happen once, 10 times, or even 1000 times, but the effort involved in the data collection is the same because the square is filled in after the first occurrence of the behavior. This approach can save a great deal of time and improve the efficiency of additional, perhaps more intensive, observation methods by allowing the observer to identify the times of the day the behavior is mostly likely to occur and thus be observable. A second benefit is that it also illustrates the time(s) of the day during which the behavior does not occur. Observations should also occur in environments that do not predict the occurrence of the behavior because they may reveal what activities, items, people and other factors foster the absence of the problem behavior, and perhaps the performance of more adaptive behaviors.

Once the time periods in which the behavior is most likely to occur have been identified, more intensive observations can be carried out in a more efficient manner. There are many formats for gathering functional assessment observation data. A few of these formats, beginning with the most basic, are described here. Educators are encouraged to view these data collection methods as examples that can be adapted to meet the specific needs of the situation.

Behavior Log

Behavior logs are among the most basic forms used to gather narrative data describing the context in which the behavior occurs. At a minimum, behavior logs should include columns for recording the antecedent, behavior, and consequences involved in a specific behavioral episode. They can also be expanded to include the date, time, activity, antecedent, problem behavior, consequences, and staff comments. It is important that behavior logs are filled out in a way that accurately describes the precursors to the behavior, the behavior itself, and the consequences that occurred immediately following the behavior. The key is to be descriptive, yet also objective and as accurate as possible. A column may be included for staff provide their insights into what happened.

Observation Format from the Functional Assessment Handbook

As described in the interview section, O'Neill and colleagues (1997) developed one of the most innovative direct observation formats available. This tool allows the observer to record and link each specific behavioral event, its environmental predictors, the perceived function, and actual consequences by simply recording a number in the appropriate columns under each section.

Another considerable strength of this format is that it is designed to be used along with the interview process. It is this author's opinion that the detailed explanations, multiple examples, comprehensiveness, and user-friendly qualities of this interview and observation format make it the most useful resource for functional assessment available at this time.

Phase 4: Getting the Most Out of the Data

Collecting meaningful data is one step in the process of functional assessment. The next critical step is conducting a thorough analysis of the data to develop a solid understanding of the contributing factors and function(s) of the student's behavior. The strategies described below can significantly strengthen the ability of educators to use assessment data to develop highly individualized and effective support plans and interventions.

First, the evaluator(s) should compare the data from questionnaires and observations for similarities and differences. As mentioned previously, there are important advantages to using multiple methods to collect data, such as interview/questionnaires and observations. The assessor can begin by comparing the findings for consistency. If the observational data supports the information gained from a questionnaire, the assessor can be more confident about the accuracy of the assumptions made concerning why certain behaviors occur.

The second step consists of searching the data for additional information that can be used to gain a better understanding of the student's behavior. Information that is not apparent from one form of data collection is sometimes derived from one form of data collection that was not apparent through the other. Such information is often not in conflict with previously gathered data; it just adds new information and creates a better understanding of the student's behavior and the context(s) in which it occurs. For example, in the questionnaire a teacher may identify a particular peer as an antecedent to a student's aggressive behavior. Observation data may indicate that, in fact, that two or three students serve as antecedents to that student's behavior; the student originally identified by the teacher plus two others. Additional information such as this does not negate the data from the questionnaire; it allows for a more complete and accurate behavioral assessment.

A third step consists of summarizing the data in each functional assessment category. During this step evaluators examine all the data with an emphasis on how different personal, family, and environmental variables (including consequences) interact to cause and maintain problem behavior. Brief case studies with a breakdown of three behavioral episodes can be found in the Appendix. These case studies further illustrate how the concepts and terms discussed in this section interact, and how the data can be organized for the purpose of summarizing results from functional assessments.

Phase 5: Develop Plausible Hypotheses or Explanations for the Occurrence of the Problem Behavior

Phase 5 is the summary stage of the functional assessment. Ultimately, the assessment team will analyze the data and develop statements that identify and explain what environmental factors and antecedents are setting the stage for or triggering the problem behavior, what consequences are reinforcing the problem behavior, and the functions being served by the problem behavior. It is good practice to have a team of two or three individuals who know the student well and are familiar with the functional assessment process examine the data and develop the explanations. It is very possible that the team members will identify a number of possible environmental factors as well as potential functions for the student's behavior.

The MAS results in scores that indicate which function(s) the student's behavior is serving for him or her. The O'Neill et al. (1997) handbook provides a number of methods evaluators can use to plot the environmental factors, antecedents, behaviors, consequences, and functions of the student's behavior. As stated earlier, this handbook is an excellent tool for relatively novice practitioners or experienced consultants seeking to conduct comprehensive functional assessments.

Optional Phase 6: Conduct a Functional Analysis

In most situations, a comprehensive functional assessment will provide the information necessary to develop an effective behavioral support plan. In some cases, however, a functional analysis may be necessary to verify the accuracy of the explanations for problem behavior developed from the functional assessment process. This step is often referred to as hypothesis or explanation testing, conducting environmental manipulations, or simply verification (Carr et al., 1994; O'Neill et al., 1997).

Functional analysis involves systematically manipulating environmental precursors of problem behavior and/or maintaining consequences identified through the functional assessment process. This step is used in situations where there is still significant uncertainty about the accuracy of the explanations that have been derived. In addition, the previously developed explanations for the occurrence of problem behavior may have led to the development of interventions and supports that are not effective. This may require the evaluator or team to go back and search or test for different explanations.

A functional analysis is then conducted to "test" each explanation until the important environmental factors and most probable function(s) are verified. An example of a functional analysis process is presented in the scenario that follows.

Example of a Functional Analysis Manipulation

Joe is a student with autism. Each day Joe yells out during lunch. Based on data from a previously completed functional assessment, his teacher is confident that Joe is yelling out to escape the noise of the busy cafeteria. The teacher wants to verify this function because he does not want to remove Joe from the cafeteria. He believes it is important that Joe have as many opportunities to interact with his peers as possible. Based on this scenario the teacher can make two explanation statements concerning Joe's behavior. One is that the noise in the cafeteria is the antecedent to Joe's yelling, and second, that the purpose of Joe's yelling is to escape the noise. This would be particularly true if Joe had been removed from the cafeteria when he yelled (negative reinforcement). By having Joe eat his lunch during a less crowded lunch period his teacher can test this explanation. Joe's teacher follows a four-step functional analysis process.

Step 1. Get an accurate baseline of Joe's behavior under the crowded cafeteria conditions. This was already accomplished during the previous functional assessment.

Step 2. Have Joe eat lunch during the less crowded period over a five-day period.

Step 3. Observe Joe's behavior during the less crowded lunch period. If Joe does not yell out or yells out significantly less often during the less crowded period, it can be assumed that the explanation of the noise serving as an antecedent and escape was accurate. This would be the end of the assessment in most scenarios involving students in school settings; however, it is common practice in functional analysis to return to the baseline situation as described in the next step.

Step 4. Joe returns to eating lunch in the cafeteria during the original busy period. If Joe yells out again, the explanation of escape being the function of Joe's behavior is further confirmed.

Note that the evaluator and team would have to weigh the benefits of exposing Joe to the busy cafeteria period again in Step 4 simply for the purpose of further verification. In most school situations this return to the original context is not necessary and questionable from an ethical standpoint.

At this point the functional analysis stage would end, and the support plan would be further developed or revised and implemented. Given the scenario above, part of that plan would include having Joe eat lunch during the quieter lunch period. Teaching Joe a more socially appropriate means for communicating his desire to leave or escape a situation in which he is not comfortable would also be an important intervention.

There are a variety of strategies, methods, and instruments for conducting functional assessments and functional analysis, but they all share the principles of applied behavior analysis as the theoretical foundation upon which they rest. Knowledge of this foundation will greatly enhance the evaluators' ability to collect meaningful assessment data, analyze it thoroughly and accurately, and draw reasonable, plausible conclusions in the form of explanations for a student's challenging behavior. The process outlined in this section is meant to serve as a guide for educators new to the functional assessment process. It can and should be altered to meet the unique needs and circumstances of the context in which it is being conducted.

Section VI

Conclusion

The usefulness of functional assessment to address challenging behavior is well documented. Increasingly, it is being used as a primary strategy for assessing student behavior in schools. As mentioned previously, perhaps the most striking benefit of functional assessment to educators is that the information derived from the assessment lends itself to the development of interventions that focus on the teaching of new skills that serve the same function as the challenging behavior. The goal is not simply to reduce or eliminate problem behavior. Functional assessment leads to the creation of learning environments that support positive student behavior. Most importantly, it provides new, more effective means for meeting the needs of teachers with students who exhibit challenging behaviors. Functional assessment helps teachers do what they do best—teach!

.

Appendix

Functional Assessment Scenarios

Each of the three scenarios presented here is a snapshot taken from a functional assessment. By themselves they are not adequate for drawing explanations about the causes of the behavior or the type of behavioral supports each student would require. The scenarios do illustrate how functional assessment data is summarized using the major categories discussed in this booklet. Ultimately the evaluator would look a many instances of problem behavior seeking patterns that provide a better understanding of student's problem behavior upon which explanations can be built.

SCENARIO 1

Mark

Ten-year old Mark left for school agitated because his parents were arguing over their shortage of money to pay the bills that month. Mark was so upset he skipped breakfast. He also forgot to take is allergy medications. Mark's allergies had him feeling drained by third period. At the beginning of this period Mark's class went to the library. His classmates were pushing and shoving in the hall. Although no one pushed Mark, a couple of students started teasing him. Mark looked around for his teacher, but she had stopped in at the office. Finally, Mark turned around and punched the teasing student who was closest to him. Somewhat shocked by Mark's aggression all of the students became quiet, including the students who were teasing Mark.

Family Factors	Personal Factors	School Factors	Antecedents	Problem Behavior(s)	Function/ Maintaining Consequences
Parents Arguing	Allergies No breakfast Fatigue	Unstructured transition	Teasing from peers	Punches the teasing student	Escape: Teasing stops

This scenario suggests the need for someone to discuss the impact of difficulties at home on Mark. The impact of not taking his medication on educational and behavioral concerns also needs to be addressed. There also appears to be a need to consider training in anger management and peer relationships.

SCENARIO 2

Marcy

Marcy is an eighth-grade student with a serious learning disability. She is quite shy and has few friends. Marcy has the most difficulty in her math class. The math teacher is reluctant to make instructional modifications for Marcy's learning disability, as a result Marcy is usually unable to follow what is going on in class and often feels lost. Today, her teacher asked Marcy to answer a question. Not knowing the answer, Marcy gave an incorrect response. Marcy's teacher told her she needed to start paying attention or she was going to flunk math. In response, Marcy said that she was doing the best she could in a loud voice. A few of the students in the class laughed and gave her the "thumbs-up" sign after her outburst.

Family Factors	Function/ Personal Factors	School Factors	Antecedents	Problem Behavior(s)	Maintaining Consequences
None Apparent	Learning disability	Lack of accommodation Unable to understand directions	Reprimand from teacher for LD	Yells at teacher	Attention: Peers laugh/ thumbs up

In this scenario, Marcy may learn that one way to impress her classmates is to act inappropriately in class. This is a fairly common situation for students with learning disabilities whose primary educational needs are not met. This scenario illustrates the need for appropriate instructional modifications related to her learning disability and assistance in using more appropriate social skills to develop friendships.

SCENARIO 3
Whitney

Whitney is a 14 year-old student who has a history of being left on her own since a young age. Whitney typically comes to school in clothing that is old, tattered and dirty or inappropriate for the season. Whitney is often absent from school. Phone calls to her home are met with indifference. When asked why she missed school Whitney will say that she overslept or that she was sick and that missing school is "no big deal" to her parents. There have always been reports that she eats an unusually unhealthy diet. Today many of these factors were in place. Whitney's parents had been out of town for the past three days. She had been skipping school and was behind in her work. Whitney was asked to do some independent work in science, but because she had missed so much school she did not have any idea what he was being asked to do. After a few minutes of staring at the worksheet, Whitney crumpled it up and threw it away. The science teacher, being sensitive to Whitney's situation, gave Whitney a new worksheet and helped her get started.

Family Factors	Personal Factors	School Factors	Antecedents	Problem Behavior(s)	Function/ Maintaining Consequences
None Apparent	Frequent absence Behind in schoolwork	Independent science work	Difficult science	Crumples worksheet and throws it away	Attention: Teacher assists with work

The larger issues in this scenario revolve around Whitney's home situation. This would certainly be an area the educational team would need to address in some way. More specific to this instance, Whitney's behavior resulted in a positive outcome for her. A concern would be that she does not use a more appropriate strategy or behavior for getting help. Although, this is only one instance, repeated scenario's similar to this would indicated that one component of a program for Whitney might include social skills instruction around asking for assistance.

References and Resources

LIST OF REFERENCES

Artesani, A. J., & Maller, L. (1998). Combining positive behavior supporters in general education settings: Combining person-centered planning and functional analysis. *Intervention in School and Clinic*, 33(1), 33–38.

Carr, E. G., Levin, L., McConnachie, G., Carlson, J. I., Kemp, D. C., & Smith, C. E. (1994). Communication-based intervention for Problem Behavior: *A user's guide for producing positive change*. Baltimore: Paul H. Brookes.

Durand, V. M., & Crimmins, D. B. (1988). *Motivation assessment scale*. Monaco & Associates Inc. Topeka, KS. Retrieved Apr. 15, 20000, from the World Wide Web: http://www.monacoassociates.com/mas/mashome.html

Durand, V. M., & Crimmins, D. B. (1988). Identifying the variables maintaining self-injurious behavior. *Journal of Autism and Developmental Disorders*, 18(1), 99–117.

Foster-Johnson, L., & Dunlap, G. (1993). Using functional assessment to develop effective, individualized interventions for challenging behaviors. *Teaching Exceptional Children, 25*(3), 44–50.

Kaplan, J. S. (1995). *Beyond behavior modification: A cognitive-behavioral approach to behavior management in the school (3rd Ed.)*. *Austin,* TX: Pro ED.

O'Neill, R. E., Horner, R. H., Albin, R. W., Sprague, J. R., Storey, K., & Newton, J. S. (1997) *Functional assessment and program development for problem behavior: A practical handbook.* (2nd Ed.). Pacific Grove, CA: Brooks/Cole.

Reichle, J., Wacker, D. (Eds.). (1993). *Communicative alternatives to challenging behavior: Integrating functional assessment and intervention strategies.* Baltimore: Paul H. Brookes.

Touchette, P. E., MacDonald, R. F., & Langer, S. N. (1985). A scatterplot for identifying stimulus control of problem behavior. *Journal of Applied Behavior Analysis, 18,* 343–351.

INTERNET RESOURCES RELATED TO STUDENT BEHAVIOR

http://www.air-dc.org/cep/resources/problembehavior/introduction.htm
CEP. (1988). *Addressing student problem behavior: An IEP Team's introduction to functional behavioral assessment and behavior intervention plans.* Washington, DC: Center for Effective Collaboration and Practice.

www.oslc.org/
The Organ Social Learning Center

http://www.cec.sped.org/osep/recon.htm
School-wide Behavioral Management Systems

http://www.cec.sped.org/bk/focus/specfoc.htm
Many links to discipline issues IDEA 97-Discipline

http://www.cec.sped.org/osep/art2.htm
Affective Behavioral Support
Expanding Placement Options
Unified Discipline
School-wide Discipline

http://darkwinguoregon.edu~ivdb/index.html
The Institute on Violence and Destructive Behavior, Community Based Prevention and Intervention University of Organ

http://www.state.ky.us/agencies/behave/homepage.html/
or
http://www.state.ky.us/agencies/behave/links.html
Kentucky Department of Education & University of Kentucky

http://interact.uoregon.edu/ss/ss.html
Institute on Violence and Destructive Behavior School Safety Project

http://amug.org/~a203/tablecontents.hml

http://www.reachoflouisville.comDocs from old webposbehav2.htm
Positive Behavior Management Principals

http://www.air-dc.or/cecp/guide/websites.htm
Web sites related to school safety and violence prevention

ADDITIONAL RESOURCES
RELATED TO STUDENT BEHAVIOR

Carr, E. G., & Durand, V. M. (1985). Reducing behavior problems through functional communication training. *Journal of Applied Behavior Analysis, 18, 111–126.*

Demchak, M. A., & Bossert, K. W. (1996). Assessing problem behaviors. In D. Browder (Ed.), *Innovations: American Association on Mental Retardation Research to Practive Series, 4* [special issue].

Donnellan, A. M., Mirenda, P. L., Mesaros, R. A., & Fassbender, L. L. (1984). Analyzing the communicative functions of aberrant behavior. *Journal of the Association of Persons with Severe Handicaps, 9,* 201–212.

Dunlap, G., Kern, L., dePerczel, M., Clarke, S., Wilson,D., Childs, K. E., White, R., & Falk, G. D. (1993). Functional analysis of classroom variables for students with emotional and behavioral disorders. *Behavioral Disorders,* 18 275–291.

Durand, V. M. (1990). *Severe behavior problems: A functional communication training approach.* New York: Guilford.

Durand, V. M. (1993). Functional assessment and functional analysis. In M. D. Smith (Ed.). *Behavior modification for exceptional children and youth.* Boston: Andover Medical Publishers.